Amazon Audible Audiobooks

Reading with Ears

Disclaimer

No part of this eBook may be transmitted or reproduced in any form including print, electronic, photocopy, scanning, mechanical or recording without prior permission from the author.

The information contained in this eBook is provided for educational purposes only.

The author has made all efforts to ensure the information contained herein is authentic. However, the author cannot be held responsible for any damage of personal or commercial nature occurring due to the misinterpretation or misrepresentation of the information. All readers are encouraged to seek professional advice as and when required. The author cannot be held responsible for any charges under any circumstances.

Summary

The world around us have revolutionized to an enormous extent. While it was imperative in the earlier ages to undertake a journey of thousand miles in order to meet a beloved residing in another continent, it is now possible to do the same via internet in a matter of minutes. In much the same way, the traditional hobby of "reading" have changed a lot – initially, the pages turned into computer and tablet screens, and now it is even possible to hear the books while on the go.

Contained in the following pages is a walk through this new technology and all that is attached with it. Keep reading to know more about Audiobooks, specifically about Amazon Audible Audiobooks.

Contents

Introduction

The art of reading and writing has developed significantly since the time it was first introduced as a medium of communication. While the earliest uses were restricted to recording information to pass it on to the future generations, it later developed into a full-fledged hobby. As a number of writing styles emerged to meet the aesthetics of readers, writing found purposes beside records – it was used to construct pieces which served the purpose of information and entertainment.

There are millions of libraries in the world with zillions of books, all containing unique content. Some of these books are very old, inscribed by authors well in the past. Some of these are new and influenced by a distinctive streak of modernity. All these books await their readers. The major issue in maintaining these libraries is trying to preserve the printed or hand-written books. With technological advancements, these problems found unmatched solutions.

The experience of reading was highly modified with the introduction of online libraries and dedicated tablet readers like Kindle. This means all information is accessible with just a 'touch'. Online libraries like Amazon.com, Google Books, Forgottenbooks.org, Questia.com and several others are leaders of this field. In other words, it is now possible to shrink entire libraries and carry them around in your pockets. Not only is it easy to carry, it is also highly affordable and competitively priced.

The first decade of 21ˢᵗ century witnessed further transformation of the reading experience in entirety. It is now possible for you to "read the books through your ears". This novel concept has been developed to improve the traditional modes of reading that allow the lovers of written word to read while on the move. Keep reading to find out more about the awesome innovation of this century.

What are Audiobooks?

Audiobooks emerged as a means to "give voice to the written words". Simply put, it is the audible version of books. It is therefore possible for you to listen to your favorite authors while you are on the move.

In the earlier ages, it was common to record plays and poetry in voice formats. The concept of Audiobooks emerged in the 1980s when book retailers were drawn to the idea of "spoken books". Since then, it developed continuously and emerged as a full-drawn medium in less than half a century.

Several of Hollywood's finest professional narrators and, at times, the authors themselves lend their voice expressions in the formation of Audiobooks. Coupled with relevant background music, an Audiobook is highly capable of giving life to the scenarios etched in the books – it is only short of a pictorial representation.

All over the world, Audiobooks are liked for the exceptionally competitive pricing, the ease of carrying it around on handheld gadgets and convenience. So if for some reason – like driving or while doing your household chores – you cannot read the books from your favorite authors, there is no reason why you cannot listen to them. Audiobooks ensure that while you have all the reason to forego reading books, you can still acquire all the information contained within them.

Brief History

Audible.com was originally created in 1995 by a thoughtful innovator Donald Katz. Audible was able to create and promote the first digital audio player well before the introduction of iPod. It was designed as a strategy to promote readership and to provide serious and non-serious readers with an alternative to reading. It is headquartered in Newark, New Jersey since 2007. Over time, it was able to gain popularity and widespread approval among the literate societies all over the world.

It was publicly traded on NASDAQ until it was finally acquired by Amazon in 2008. It now enjoys the status of being an Amazon subsidiary, accredited as the largest online Audiobooks library and the unparalleled monopolistic leader in this field.

With time, Amazon has been able to improve greatly on the offerings of Audible.com in order to further enhance the customer experiences. At present, it not only offers the readers/listeners with an opportunity to listen on a wide array of personal gadgets, it is also able to provide the authors a $1/sale incentive which is readily convertible into $20 million. It has branched out into three platforms – audible.com, audible.co.uk and iTunes – which guarantee profitable returns to the authors.

Currently, audible.com has over 100,000 Audiobooks to choose from, authored by more than 1200 different writers, which amounts to more than 1,000,000 hours of audio. The content contains books, radio shows, speeches, stand-up comedy, interviews, periodicals and magazines. It can therefore be regarded as an extensive library of Audiobooks, well capable of meeting the specific tastes of different readers.

Benefits of Audible Audiobooks

There are numerous advantages attached with Audiobooks. The foremost is their contribution towards inculcating the love for books. Audiobooks are a convenient mode of promoting literacy. While you may not have the time or the heart to read the books/magazines you need to, listening to them makes the feat easier and more rewarding. The list does not end here – for specific groups, the advantages have been identified in the following headings.

For Children

Children are one of the best mimickers – whatever they see they try to imitate just that. The Audiobooks are therefore an unparalleled resource in helping them build their expressions.

The play in voice is exceptionally exaggerated in children's Audiobooks. This helps them acknowledge the content in a proper manner, understand the specific voice expressions and their usage, and also to learn and repeat it in similar situations. It is therefore no surprise that the oldest known records of Audiobooks comprise of children's plays and stories.

For Teenagers

Audiobooks are known to impact the intermediate learners group as positively as the children. The teenagers can be coached to use the books for greater benefits without being put through the tedious and, at times, offensive task of reading them. This includes:

1. Promotion of critical reading (or listening to be more appropriate) and comprehension,
2. Increasing vocabulary,
3. Building accents and spoken styles,
4. Familiarize with foreign languages,
5. Improving speaking and writing skills,
6. Introducing them to rare or advanced genres,
7. Enhancing imagination and visualization skills.

In fact, it has been supported by research that listening helps readers in visualizing the scenarios more effectively than reading them off the pages.

Furthermore, Audiobooks can help teenagers initiate meaningful discussions and debates with elders if it is played, for instance, in the car, audible to the teenager and elder at the same time. This encourages critical evaluation of the information contained in the Audiobooks and is likely to help the teenager become intelligent, sharp and evaluative.

For Adults

The benefits of Audiobooks for adults have already been highlighted previously. It allows the hardcore readers to read more in the given time span. Moreover, it also helps those on the way to becoming hardcore readers get into the habit. So while adults commute to and from their workplaces or while driving across to a different city to meet a relative, an Audiobook can prove to be an educational and productive company. It allows you to gain information you may want or need in the most convenient manner. Even while you cook those delectable recipes in the kitchen, an Audiobook can help you get the right ingredients together!

For adults, the Audiobooks have advanced benefits as compared with those for children and young adults. It has nevertheless proved to be a fruitful solution for those readers who just cannot find time in their busy schedules to dedicate to this hobby. So while you are on the move, you can still listen to your favorite authors.

For Handicapped

Last but not the least; Audiobooks can greatly help the handicapped. It is known to help individuals that are:

1. Blind or possess limited sight
2. Dyslexic
3. ADHD
4. Limited mobility

These individuals cannot enjoy the reading experience in the traditional way. However, Audiobooks allow them to get the feel of the book in a unique manner which puts them equal to those without handicap. The world of technological advancements has created opportunities for everyone. Being a handicap does not necessarily restrict the person on his or her acquisition of information and knowledge. Audiobooks ensures every single person is provided with equal opportunities of excelling regardless of what the nature decided for them.

Apparently, the uses and benefits of Audiobooks are plenty. You have been introduced with the concept and ideology behind Audiobooks and are now fully aware of how these can impact you and your lifestyle. Keep reading to find out how you can indulge yourself with the Audiobooks available at Audible.com, an Amazon subsidiary.

Getting Started

If you have been convinced about the importance and usability of Audiobooks and you are looking for a place to get started, you have reached your desired destination. Contained in this section is a detailed tour about how to acquire Audiobooks and how to listen to them on your preferred gadget. All you need is an internet connection, a credit card or some medium to pay Amazon for the Audiobooks and some good quality headphones!

Free Audiobooks

Nothing beats a free trial. At Amazon Audible, you get the first free taste which is likely to get you hitched for years to come.

Sign In

How it Works   About Membership   Search for a great book

Download a
free Audiobook

Listen to one of our top best sellers or choose from 150,000+ other titles

GET A FREE DOWNLOAD

Sign in with your **amazon** account.

Audible Free Trial Details
Get an audiobook of your choice, free, with a 30-day trial. After the trial, your paid membership will begin at $14.95 per month. With your membership, you will receive one credit every month, good for any audiobook on Audible.

All you need to do is log on to Audible.com or Audible.co.uk (according to the place you live in or the accent you would like to hear the books in) – you will be greeted with this exciting offer right on the homepage. Clicking on the "Get a free download" tab will prompt you for your email address and password (in case you already have an Amazon account). As a new user, you will need to select the option "No, I am new Amazon customer" before clicking "Continue".

We're an Amazon company.

Sign in using your Amazon account.

My e-mail address is: [   ]

Do you have an Amazon.com password?

○ Yes, my Amazon password is: [   ]

◉ No, I am a new Amazon customer.   Forgot password?

CONTINUE

It will ask you for some personal details and register your new free account. You can then access their Audiobooks library and select the one you would like to try. It is important to keep in mind that the free-trial covers thirty days in total. On the expiry of this period, your paid membership of $14.95 per month will be initiated automatically. If you choose to discontinue before this period, you will be charged no cost at all.

A membership with Amazon's Audible can be extremely rewarding as you can earn discounts and promotional offers based on the frequency of your use. This means the free trial is most likely to make you a long-term user at Audible.

Samples and Links

Amazon Audible Audiobooks allow you to preview the books up to ten minutes in a block. Moreover, you can share these previews on your social networking profiles like Facebook and Twitter in order to inform your contacts about the most recent book you are listening to. This promotes intellectual discussions and debates about different aspects of the book. This also allows you to get feedback and reviews about a particular book before investing your time and money into it. The samples and links allow you to integrate the social element into your book reading/listening ventures.

How to Purchase Audiobooks from Audible.com

Purchasing Audiobooks at Audible.com is a simple task. The only thing you need is a valid credit card or a medium to pay for your purchases. It is better to opt for memberships which allow you to download a certain number of books per month. There are different membership packages to meet different "reading" frequencies of users.

All you need to do is to search the online library for books of your choice, put them in the cart and download it on your preferred gadgets to start enjoying the read instantly! If the book is not according to your aesthetics, you can opt for a refund as well. Audible.com will help you navigate through the library and find the books you would like so that your user experience is exemplary.

Downloading

Downloading is an easy feat. You can easily download your Audiobooks on your favorite portable gadgets so that you can carry it around anywhere you go. The records of your personal Audiobooks library are stored with your online Amazon account. This means you can access your Audiobooks from anywhere using your online account.

However, the first time you try to access your library from a different gadget, it can prove to be tricky. Certain restrictions have been imposed on the number of devices the library can be used on in order to prevent the infringement of copyrights and piracy. Once the Audible store associates your gadgets with the account, you can access your Amazon library anytime, anywhere, any number of times that you need to.

Currently, the Amazon Audiobooks are compatible with laptops, computers, audio players, smart phones, a wide range of Kindles and streaming media devices. You can download the Audiobooks directly on your devices using Wi-Fi connectivity, if available.

In case your device does not support wireless connectivity, the Audiobooks can be downloaded on your computer and then transferred onto your portable gadget. The file format for Audible Audiobooks is ".aa" or ".aax" – it is therefore important for you to figure out whether your device is capable of playing this specific format.

Especially for AudibleAir – downloading Audiobooks wirelessly over Wi-Fi connection – it is possible to optimize the memory usage of your device. You can opt for Amazon's advanced features which downloads new chapters on your device and deletes the old ones you have listened to so that your device memory is not overloaded.

With recent advancements, it is also possible to synchronize multiple devices so that you can switch between them seamlessly. This has been covered in detail under the heading "Whispersync".

Sharing

Amazon Audible has strict policies in order to prevent the infringement of copyrights and to discourage piracy. All Audible Audiobooks are protected by Digital Rights Management (DRM) protocol which does not allow the sharing or distribution of the downloaded material. The content cannot be stored or distributed in any way. The violation of this condition can be subjected with legal perusal and actions. This particular policy has been criticized sternly in the past decade. It has previously caused problems and issues as well. However, the problems have been resolved and the DRM protocol has been relaxed a little due to which customer grievances have declined. It is therefore possible for you to access your Audiobooks on multiple devices from the same account.

The Library

The Amazon's Audible is an extensive store of Audiobooks pertaining to different genres and categories. It is known to have over thousands of books in each category which ensures there is something for everyone. This also means there is ample choice available in terms of titles, so once you are done with one specific book, you can find similar titles almost immediately. All age groups and all major interests have been covered in the Amazon Audible library.

If this is not enough, the Amazon Audible library is dedicated to provide continued services. For this reason, hundreds of titles are added on a monthly basis to cater to the customer requirement of something new. The bestsellers also become available readily on Audible which proves to be unparalleled in terms of value and entertainment.

The Amazon Audible Audiobooks are available in all major categories like Children's books, Classics, Fiction, Romance, Business, Mystery, Biographies and Memoirs, and Self-Empowerment. This section contains some information about these respective categories.

Children's Books

There are over ten thousand titles in this category which continue to increase day by day due to Amazon's persistence in enlarging the library. This extensive library is further divided according to the children's ages and according to the specific topics of the books like fiction, classics, fairytales, nonfiction and mysteries. For school going children, Amazon hosts a number of study guides to help them prepare for their examinations and perform wonderfully in them.

Kids   View All 11913 Kids Titles >>

Ages 0-4 (1264)	Ages 5-7 (5604)	Ages 8-10 (6619)	Animal Stories (1839)
Biographies & History (449)	Classics (1134)	Fables, Fairy Tales & Myths (860)	Fiction (6891)
Mysteries (533)	Nonfiction (497)	Sci-Fi & Fantasy (1187)	Study Guides (55)
With Synchronized Images (303)			

The homepage highlights the most popular Audiobooks and also contains reviews from those who have experienced it. It is very rare to see a negative feedback from any customer; however, it is not entirely absent. Nevertheless, the reviews can give an idea about what to expect when you have paid and downloaded the specific Audiobook.

There is a suggestion bar containing the trending Audiobook titles. These books are the ones which are increasingly becoming popular or have received outstanding reviews.

Furthermore, there is a list of suggestions containing the bestseller titles and the new releases which can help you lay your hands on the newest titles and experience the new before several others.

Classics

The classics are undoubtedly an unparalleled source of literature and knowledge. At Amazon Audible, there are more than six thousand titles in this category. As with the children's books, this category is further divided into sub-categories including American Literature, British Literature, European Literature, World Literature and a specific designated category for Shakespeare's contributions.

Classics

View All 6364 Classics Titles >>

American Literature (1488)	British Literature (2376)	Drama (143)	European Literature (923)
Greek & Roman (170)	Kids & Young Adults (281)	Nonfiction (159)	Poetry (406)
Shakespeare (306)	World Literature (680)		

The suggestions and new releases exist in this category as well which allows you to investigate new topics and titles, and be the first one to review it. If adventure is not exactly your "style", you can always opt for titles which have already received customer reviews.

Audiobooks are an effective way of creating attraction in classics. This genre is quite unpopular in terms of understanding and general interest. With Audiobooks, it is possible for teachers and parents to introduce the youth towards this world of knowledge in a better manner which makes them appreciate it and consider it for future perusal.

Fiction

It feels nice to retreat into the world of imagination every once in a while amidst foreign creatures and weird laws of nature. This genre serves this purpose – a short escape from reality which allows you to relax in the foreign land. At Audible, there over twenty thousand titles in this genre which can be further classified into eleven categories.

Fiction

View All 23359 Fiction Titles >>

African-American (480)	Chick Lit (1458)	Contemporary (9015)	Gay & Lesbian (375)
Historical (4358)	Horror (1716)	Humor (884)	Literary (2967)
Religious & Inspirational (1452)	Short Stories & Anthologies (3717)	Westerns (1228)	

This genre at Audible is exceptionally impressive with several award-winning Audiobooks showcased on the homepage. The suggestion list here is quite extensive covering several eye-catching titles that will make you purchase all these in one go.

There are several fiction books which have been voiced over by renowned Hollywood stars and several highly rated professional narrators. This promises to make the "reading" experience especially rewarding for you.

Romance

It feels great to step out of your own problem-filled story and step into someone else's love story which has been perfected to the last bit. Authors of romantic books are exceptionally skilled in heightening expectations and increasing dissatisfaction in relationships. Nevertheless, these books are almost always close to heart and reality, free from alien elements and quite relatable.

At Audible, there are over six thousand titles in this genre, each promising to be a one-of-a-kind "read".

Romance   View All 6884 Romance Titles >>

| Chick Lit (201) | Contemporary (2799) | Erotica (186) | Fantasy (1286) |
| Historical (1610) | Religious & Inspirational (372) | Suspense (1195) | |

There are numerous options in terms of bestseller and new release suggestions. New sub-categories are also being introduced with time in order to cater the specific tastes of users. Some authors and narrators have produced series of Audiobooks which provide continuity and uninterrupted story flow.

Business

The experienced have a lot to share about transforming your struggles into distinguished successes. While often there is no singular technique which applies to everyone and yields the same victorious results, these books undoubtedly serve as a source of motivation and inspiration to continue toiling with your work even if you face a couple of failures. There may even be some people for whom these business practices can actually yield the desired results.

At Audible, this genre is a popular one with over seven thousand titles already present in the library. There is no aspect of business which is left unattended.

Business

View All 7555 Business Titles >>

Career Skills (2251)	Commerce & Economy (2871)	Leadership (1544)	Management (1892)
Marketing (560)	Personal Finance & Investing (751)	Sales (349)	

The new arrivals and popular suggestions are continually updated with unique variety. For strugglers, would-be entrepreneurs and business managers, this genre is of immense significance. It serves to keep you on the right track which leads to sure success. Audiobooks are exceptionally productive as the listeners of this specific genre seldom have time to read the written word. Thus its utility is quite pronounced.

Mystery

Often the biggest mystery is when an important character drops dead all of a sudden and there are simply too many suspects or none to blame. It is quite capable of keeping you excited and engrossed, guessing the unpredictable story plot while you are always on your toes. These thrills are your escape from a monotonous reality.

At Audible, there are over eighteen thousand titles which promise to keep you on your toes, listening to the entire Audiobook in a single sitting.

Mysteries & Thrillers

View All 18417 Mysteries & Thrillers Titles >>

Classic Detective (1273)	Espionage (1026)	Historical (1296)	Legal Thrillers (618)
Medical Thrillers (298)	Modern Detective (6510)	Noir (349)	Police Procedurals (660)
Radio Dramas (269)	Suspense (11722)	True Crime (266)	

Several titles are added into this genre quite frequently. The suggestions lists are quite widespread for this category as well. This means you can have one nail biting experience after another. It is also possible to browse entire collections pertaining to your favorite authors and listen to them one-by-one so that the sequence of events is undisturbed and the subsequent Audiobooks make perfect sense. There is no reason why your thrilling and numbing journeys should ever end!

Biographies and Memoirs

Everyone's life is unique but the lives of some people are truly spectacular. The events and happenings of their lives is a tale to cherish. It serves as a lesson, an inspiration and a resource for guidance. A biography is the detailed description and account of one's life. It covers more than just basic achievements – the person can talk about the main events which determined the course of action his/her life took. For the renowned and cherished celebrities, the reader's fervor is exceptionally advanced.

At Audible, there are over seven thousand biographies and memoirs preserved in voice format pertaining to different celebrities and professionally accomplished individuals.

Bios & Memoirs

View All 7935 Bios & Memoirs Titles >>

Artists, Writers, & Musicians (1488)	Business Leaders (389)	Celebrities (1261)	Criminals (150)
Personal Memoirs (4164)	Political Figures (1134)	Religious Figures (284)	Science & Technology Leaders (240)

The library is continually updated to include new releases and best sellers. It is important to note that this category does not only include the professionally accomplished, but also highlights some people's challenging lifestyles. For instance, if an individual was diagnosed with an incurable medical problem which put the family through a test, this is also preserved in the form of a book to help other similar families get through with their challenges easily. And there is no better way than Audible to lend a listening ear to other's experiences while having one's own hands full with responsibilities.

History

The aged pages have seen and experienced more than any person can ever do in their entire lifetime. The worth of the old parchment can never be compensated with that of an extra-refined page of today. As nationalists or just some person not willing to repeat the mistakes of yester years, history serves as the connection between forefathers and the children of today. As it is popularly known, those who do not know about their history are destined to doom.

At Audible, there are over five thousand audios willing to enlighten the listener about the past.

History

View All 5580 History Titles >>

20th Century (1032)	21st Century (218)	American (2120)	Ancient (358)
European (872)	Kids & Young Adults (8)	Military (1186)	Political (512)
World (1483)			

This section is exceptionally rich in literature and knowledge. There is a lot to be rediscovered. While reading history books may be challenging for most people, listening to these brief audios promise to improve the experience significantly. You can acquire the knowledge of the ancient civilizations while driving to work. Moreover, you can find out about the history of your country and of other countries without much hassle.

Sci-fi and Fantasy

Science fiction and fantastical stories used to be a charm for children but it is now equally popular among adults. The fancy world of imagination is an easy escape from harsh realities. From another perspective, the farfetched ingenious creations portrayed in these books serve as a prototype – at some point in the future, the unimaginable does become a reality with scientific research and development.

At Audible, there are around ten thousand unique science fiction stories waiting to be heard.

Sci-Fi & Fantasy

View All 9946 Sci-Fi & Fantasy Titles >>

Doctor Who (303)	Dramatizations (470)	Fantasy: Contemporary (1470)	Fantasy: Epic (1824)
Fantasy: Paranormal (1784)	Sci-Fi: Classic (594)	Sci-Fi: Contemporary (2840)	Short Stories & Anthologies (50)
Star Trek (92)	Star Wars (168)		

New titles are continually added in this category to ensure user loyalty. It is a convenient medium to transform your surroundings anywhere and at any time. There are several well-known series included in this category. It therefore promises to be an unparalleled and easy-to-reach source of entertainment.

Self-Development

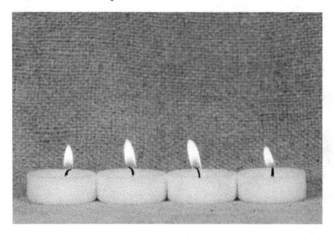

Some books are dedicated to build some specific characteristics in a person. If you want to polish your communication skills but you do not know where and how to start, you can easily find a book to help you get there. There are also some books formulated around some tips and advices to make you more productive and determined in your work – undoubtedly, the source is experience rather than contemplation.

At Audible, there are over twelve thousand Audiobooks to help you become better and accomplished individuals.

Self Development

View All 12843 Self Development Titles >>

Communication Skills (715)	How-To (3762)	Hypnosis (1238)	Meditation (960)
Motivation & Inspiration (4354)	Parenting (713)	Personal Finance (1206)	Relationships (1431)
Sexuality (632)			

No person is born perfect. There are always shortcomings which can be improved with time and effort. This section aims to address and overcome the million problems faced by different people. It is therefore a popular category with an ever-increasing library of information and knowledge pertaining to simple changes yielding long-drawn results. If reading is a challenge, listening definitely is not.

Advancing Science

There is more to the Audiobooks than simply the conversion of the written word into a voice format. The science behind the functioning of Audible is not simple. Here are a few more things you need to know about Audible before you can start enjoying the Audiobooks. Rest assured, the experience at Audible.com will be rewarding for everyone who opts for it. These few additional things can help you make the most out of your investment.

Promotional Codes

7919275 690612

Audible is an Amazon subsidiary. You can acquire promotional codes through any promotional offers launched by Audible. These codes allow you to access Audiobooks of your choice. You can also opt to convert it into Audiobooks credits at Audible. It is important for you to have an Amazon Audible account in order to retrieve the benefits from these codes. The usage and benefits of these codes is governed by local laws and may become void according to your location. Furthermore, it is important for you to read the terms and conditions thoroughly as these promotional codes are prone to expiry after a certain time period has elapsed. Additional terms and conditions as mentioned on the codes are also applicable on redemption.

Nevertheless, the promotional codes give you an unmatched opportunity to experience the world of Audiobooks without making any payments out of your pockets. If the free Audiobooks given on sign up is not enough to make up your mind about it, the promotional codes will definitely want you to keep coming back for more.

Gifts

At Audible, you can gift memberships to your loved ones so they can enjoy the Audiobooks experience as well. These memberships are competitively priced and include several additional benefits like discounts and gift credits.

The Gift Center
Give the gift that speaks volumes

Choose a Gift Membership

3	Give 3 months	$45	Give as a Gift
6	Give 6 months	$90	Give as a Gift
12	Give 12 months	$150	Give as a Gift

Gift Memberships Include:

Concierge Setup
Our staff is ready 24/7 to help gift members start listening in minutes

1 Credit Per Month
Good to use on over **150,000 titles**

Exclusive Discounts
30% off every title every day

This means you can make others experience the same excitement as yourself and introduce them to a long-lasting relationship with Audible – for the best prices. As opposed with promotional codes, these gift memberships are not prone to expiry and can be redeemed anytime, anywhere and by anyone.

Library Management

At Audible, managing your library is an easy feat. This is mainly because it is done automatically online. All Audiobooks that you purchase are routinely added to your online library. This means you can access them at any time you like. This is one reason why you can access your Audiobooks on multiple gadgets seamlessly. You user name and password are the keys to enter your library.

This serves another purpose – you do not need to download the bulky Audiobooks on your computers and gadgets or store them on your hard disk. This can prove to be very inconvenient and space occupying – leaving very less memory for other activities. With Audible online library, all Audiobooks that you purchase remain with you. So whenever you feel like listening to a specific Audiobook again, you can easily download it on your gadget and delete it once you are through with it. This will make sure you have space for downloading other and newer Audiobooks.

This online library will also help you make wise decisions and avoid purchasing an Audiobook which is already present in your library. Since the titles are displayed in front of you, you can check and select newer Audiobooks to keep you company rather than accidently buying those Audiobooks you are already through with.

"Whispersync" Synchronization

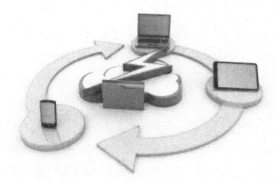

Amazon Audible is dedicated to enhance the reader's experience to the highest degree.

Whispersync Synchronization allows the reader to switch between reading and listening continuously without losing pace. This means if you are busy working in the kitchen but have managed to get that five minutes block where you can sit down and relax, you can opt to stop the audio and start reading it from exactly the same spot as where you switched off the audio. This allows enriching the user's reading experience by merging the traditional with the contemporary.

All you need to do is purchase the kindle eBook and the related professional narration audio. Once you have both, you can synchronize them easily and automatically. There is a list of devices on which the Whispersync Synchronization can be applied and used.

At the moment, there are more than 30,000 titles in the Whispersync library. New titles are being added continuously seeing the positive customer response.

Whispersync ensures your reading experience includes actual reading as well.

Immersion Reading

It is not just Whispersync Synchronization – the ability to switch between audio and reading. With Immersion reading, you can opt for both services simultaneously.

If you have time and space, and you want to have that 360 degree reading experience which can totally sweep you off your feet, then immersion reading is definitely the thing to try. While you listen to the audio, the relevant text keeps highlighting on the screen. This means you can read and listen to the text at the same time.

This can help in improving the cognitive skills considerably. Moreover, immersion reading can help develop reading habits and language skills by improving pronunciations and grammar. For children and adults, immersion reading is an exceptional learning tool.

Digital Rights Management (DRM)

The Digital Rights Management is the phenomenon practiced by Audible to protect copyrights violation. This means the Audiobooks you download cannot be stored on an external device (like burned to a CD etc.). Moreover, you cannot electronically or otherwise, share the downloaded file with devices which are not recognized as your own. This is done in order to prevent piracy and economic damage occurring thereof.

It is also possible for Audible to legally pursue any person known to violate these terms and conditions according to the extent of infringement. It is therefore advised not to try to find a way out of this obligation.

Personalization

With Audible, the complete authority lies with you. It is possible to personalize the Audiobooks according to your needs.

You can:

1. Adjust the narration speed
2. Transfer Audiobooks to your proffered gadget via Wi-Fi.
3. Navigate through different chapters.
4. Bookmark specific portions for easy access.
5. Time the narration to "sleep".
6. Download the Audiobook in the background while you perform different tasks on your device.
7. Connect to Facebook and Twitter with Audible and let your friends and contacts know about the latest Audiobook you are listening to.
8. Gain information about authors, their events and more confidential information with respect to the world of literature.

Mobile Applications

Audible has developed its mobile platform for Apple phones and for Android phones as well. This helps you to remain connected with your library at all times. You can choose to download your Audiobooks on your mobile phones via Wi-Fi connectivity.

The layout is user-friendly which allows you to access all important information right from the dashboard. The latest news and events are also displayed on the main screen allowing you to get the main highlights without hassle.

There are slightly different formats for Apple and Android versions which take into consideration the differences between the two. This means whether you have an Apple phone or an Android phone, your experience with mobile Audible will be a rewarding one.

In this era of technological aptness, developing mobile application has proved to be a fruitful investment on behalf of Audible. This allows you to access the Audiobooks anytime and anywhere, straight from your handheld phone.

Customer Support

The user interface at Audible is extremely simple and effective. Even so, if you face problems in accessing the library or making the software work for you, you can seek the technical support staff through multiple mediums. They have phone, email and mailing address available on their website in order to facilitate communications.

In addition to seeking customer support services, you can also contribute productively to the operations at Audible. You can mail in your ideas and thoughts about how to improve the services provision at Audible.

You can place request for Audiobooks – if there is a book you found extremely interesting and would love to hear to its audible version or if there is one book you need to read but cannot find the time to dedicate to it, you can inform Audible about it.

You can be heard – write testimonials and mail them to Audible so that they can publish it on their website as customer feedback. This will help other Audible customers evaluate the Audiobooks critically before purchasing.

Lastly, you can also apply for job vacancies at Audible through their "Contact Us" section. If you want to contribute your time and energy to Audible, there is nothing to stop you!

Final Word

To sum it all, Audible Audiobooks is an intelligent invention by Amazon. You can totally revolutionize your reading experiences through Audiobooks. The simple user interface and advanced customer support promises to make your experience a truly rewarding one. Moreover, Audible is one-of-a-kind service – it has no competitors. This means no one else can deliver the experience as Amazon Audible Audiobooks can.

The easy switching between gadgets is another unparalleled benefit provided by Audible. Like most other services, Audible allows you to remain completely free without being locked down. This ensures you are truly mobile while accessing Audible.

If you still need a push to begin the life-long journey with Audible, the free trial will make you decide in its favor. Log on now to http://www.audible.com or http://www.audible.co.uk and begin browsing Audiobooks right away!